T0148522

Grace Abounds

Grace Abounds

Keri Ann Unsworth

WESTBOW
PRESS®
A DIVISION OF THOMAS NELSON
& ZONDERVAN

WestBow Press books may be ordered through booksellers or by contacting:

WestBow Press
A Division of Thomas Nelson & Zondervan
1663 Liberty Drive
Bloomington, IN 47403
www.westbowpress.com
1 (866) 928-1240

ISBN: 978-1-5127-0363-4 (sc)
ISBN: 978-1-5127-0364-1 (e)

Print information available on the last page.

WestBow Press rev. date: 11/05/2016

Preface

The prompting of the Holy Spirit inspired me to take time out of life and really immerse myself in God's Word. Through the experience of surrendering the plans I had for me, the Lord began to speak to me daily during the time I spent on my knees and in His Word in prayer. From this intimate time in the Word, God began opportunities to share the word of the work He was performing in my life. Spiritual rewards overflowed as the testimony and the power of His Word through me influenced transformation in others. As I realized the word of our testimonies is one of the most powerful elements to our walk with Christ, the writing for Grace Abounds was born. The passion for sharing with young ladies the message of the power of the Cross overwhelmed me. The more time I invested in people, the more I recognized that there are a lot of people living in the pain of their past that need to be freed. The message of how faith the size of a mustard seed is the key to experiencing God's best regardless of anyone's past really burdened my heart. I want every person to understand and receive that the power of Christ IS greater in them. The experiences of His Power in my own life persuaded me to use writing as a vehicle to capture practical application of what happens when we read God's word, follow, and believe in the power of "it is written". The words that I write are purposed to share the realness of God's power and love with true life examples of His supernatural transforming power. While this book is merely a snapshot of what the Lord has done in my life and through His ministry, I believe that it will help someone recognize that they are no different than myself and they too can walk in Grace filled shoes with Christ. This book is dedicated to my entire family because without their amazing support I could not have followed through with this commitment. A special thanks to my husband, Jonathan, who is an amazing leader, husband, and father. Your persevering patience with me is critical in this journey as God pursues me to write.

About the Author

Keri Unsworth is an active leader in discipleship ministries, youth ministry, and women's ministry. Grace Abounds Ministries of South Carolina was born in 2010 when Keri was called to work with struggling families and help them transform their lives. Through this journey, Keri was sharing her own story of God's Hand on her life through online blogging. This writing and ministry are Spirit led, unpredictable, and not about her. This platform is dedicated to sharing whatever the Lord calls her to that He has shown from His word that fosters spiritual growth in life. In September of 2010, the Lord called Keri to leave her career and step out in Faith to pursue His best for her life. She is blessed with a supportive and wonderful husband, Jonathan, and a son.

Chapter One

He Made Me With A Purpose

*"I praise you because I am fearfully and wonderfully made;
your works are wonderful, I know
that full well."* Psalm 139:14

The days of my childhood brought forward distinct seasons filled with unpredictable combinations of joy, togetherness, and division. While my father was in the Marine Corps my mother delivered me on my father's birthday at Yuma Medical Center the 6th day of November of 1976.

While living in military housing in Yuma, Arizona, we were then transferred to Pascagoula, Mississippi in 1979. While there, my sister, Jimi Lynne and I grew closer, as our mother, Linda, a young Jackie Onassis look-alike, continued to maintain our home and nurture us for a healthy and productive life. My father James, a stoic handsome man, was really into his military path, but received an opportunity to fulfill his dreams to build a career with a nuclear plant in Vicksburg, Mississippi. And without a college degree he prospered in the field of computer technology. I adored (and still do!) my daddy, and to this day the smell of freshly mowed grass brings to my mind the days when our family was together. We stayed in Vicksburg for the rest of my youth.

In the house on Overlook Drive, where Jimi Lynne and I were raised, Kool-Aid and Little Debbie snacks were a staple in our house that drew the neighborhood kids to engage in multiple activities that my mom enjoyed hosting. Or, maybe it was the trampoline and the swimming pool that were the real draw. Life was comfortable. My parents enjoyed entertaining close friends through playing cards and country dancing, where our home was full of laughter, joy and love.

My daddy was always the life of the party, but when I was 9 years of age, unexplained circumstances cost my dad his job and everything changed overnight.

The yelling and screaming between my mom and dad caused the warmth of the house to subside and left Jimi Lynne and I vulnerable, insecure, and confused. Within a matter of days, our house was sold, the vehicles were sold, and our parents informed us that we would be changing schools. About this same time, my sister's best friend Sondra started inviting us to church. My parents resisted for quite some time because to them it was about "giving up" their beer and poker nights. Eventually, the persistence of my sister Jimi Lynne begging them caused them to surrender to the idea of visiting Sondra's church. And frankly, I was glad because she was driving me CRAZY! Our lives were forever impacted though by this tiny decision.

At Goodrum Baptist Church, I watched my daddy surrender his heart to Jesus. I watched the guys that followed him say, "If God can change Jimmy Holder,

Keri Ann Unsworth

then he can change me". It was similar to a swarm of party animals turning their lives over to the Lord because of what God did in the life of my father. During this time, my mom recommitted her life to the Lord, and at the age of 9 I made the decision to follow Christ as well. The presence of the Holy Spirit in our home church in the small town of Vicksburg, Mississippi transformed our family's outlook.

Even though I was only a 5th grader, I would take my Bible out at recess and share with any kid that would listen about the relationship that we needed to have with Jesus Christ. There was even a boy named Eric that wanted to be my boyfriend, but I told him that I could not be his girlfriend because he did not believe in Jesus. Turns out he was a Jehovah's witness, so a relationship with him would have been really complicated! Yet, at the age of 9 I knew I was called to be a bold disciple for Jesus without fear. Being a young girl, I feared the Lord and had a desire to pursue Him with purpose, passion and commitment.

For the next seven years we would go on to live a typical middle class lifestyle residing in a small townhome that we rented. My mom worked to supplement my father's income, but my dad worked and worked and worked sun up until sun down, feeling as if he was on a treadmill going nowhere. We lived the Southern Baptist life all the way down to the "culottes" that were definitely inspired by the enemy himself…you know those ridiculous garments that hang like a skirt, but they are actually pants. Yes, those. Yes, I wore those. I had a pair for every color of the rainbow fashioned by my mammaw – "the amazing seamstress". My sister and I were joyful kids living what we believed to be a pretty normal and ordinary life. Even though the nature of the seasons my family experienced during my youth were unpredictable, turning 16 had entirely new meaning for me because my family entered into a whirlwind of challenges that involved drastic changes that fractured the foundation of our family values.

Chapter Two

I Believed

"A Father to the fatherless..." Psalm 68:5

My sweet 16th birthday was difficult because my daddy was away on business. If you recall, I was born ON his birthday, so it was always a very special and important day for the both of us. To my surprise, he would buy me my very own pool stick, because our favorite pastime was to go to the bowling alley and shoot pool. I really believe my daddy did this to run off all potential candidates so that I would forego the idea of dating.

Shortly after returning from his trip, I would go to school and then come home to find my father's closet completely empty. The arguments that he and my mom had on a daily basis were no secret, but they seemed to always find common ground. I knew, especially when I saw the state of my daddy's closet, that this time would be different. So, I called my mom at work to tell her what I had discovered and she would ask me a lot of questions but did not seem too concerned. She said, "Oh honey, he always comes back. Do not worry!" Well, in just a matter of days, my father pulled into the driveway mad as the devil, and came inside to speak with my mom. This was a very ironic moment in my life as the Andy Griffith show was playing on the T.V. in the background as my mom and dad had a real meeting of the minds about where their marriage stood. I was in the kitchen cooking steak patties, where I stayed until the storm had passed. In half an hour, my dad left, my mom stood in the living room crying and confused, and I decided not to ask. It was over. He was gone.

The next year of high school was a complete blur. My mother cried every day. I had to get a job at Kmart to help take care of necessities. I laid in bed at night questioning, "If my Earthly father can just leave me behind like this, then how can I believe that a Sovereign Heavenly Father loves me?" I also asked, "How do I know what is the Truth? The road my father is taking defies everything I have been raised to believe, so is it all really true? Is God's word true and right?"

The belief struggle began. I did not believe that I was valuable. I did not believe that I mattered. And I sure did not have a strong belief that I mattered to God.

The next several days were very lonely. I was still somehow consumed with getting the attention of a boy who wrote me off in 8th grade. A group of girls that I had known since 1st grade seemed like a safe place to fall. I had lunch period with them. They talked about boys, sex, and drinking alcohol. A whole world opened up that was unknown to me before. My mom was working nights at the casino in the gift shop, and whenever she was home, she was shut up in her room crying. I was really angry at her for giving up on life. I would knock on her door and tell her, "Mom, you have GOT to get a life! You are not dead and you still have a purpose!"

Keri Ann Unsworth

During the process of working and crying, my mom lost A LOT of weight, but eventually she would start "getting out more". Many nights she did not come home. I realized that I could pretty much do whatever I wanted because she was not paying attention. The girls from school invited me out one night to a place my father had forbidden me to ever consider going…"across the bridge" to Louisiana where 18 year-olds can drink legally. So, one night I had nothing better to do so I went.

Hesitant, nervous, and convicted, it was the first time I went somewhere without asking for permission. For me, it was a serious departure from what my parents had taught me. I arrived at the bar and saw so many of the popular guys with girls that I knew from school. Finally, I realized why I was not sought after like some of these girls. Everything in me, which was Jesus, was different because I chose not to drink and have sex. Unfortunately, I went out a few more times and do not want to remember the details of my actions. I know that I was drinking and engaged in sex with a boy in a way that was not glorifying to God or myself. My best friend at the time was having an issue with her parents because they were also nearing the end of their own tragedy. I saw my best friend pull away from me and she started hanging with a different crowd. Her grades fell and the relationship she once had with God was no longer bearing fruit. I did not see good things happening in her life. I knew that I wanted a better life, a great life, and a fulfilled life. My mom did not attend our home church anymore, because it was too painful. I knew that I was at a crossroads between making a great life changing decision, or going downhill.

I saw the people that stayed faithful to God show real joy and peace. My best friend was walking in opposition to God's commands and she seemed miserable. So, I began to pray that the Lord, if He is real, and His Word is true, to connect me with a church that He could use to give me the support I needed. The Lord's answer was nearly immediate. I ran into an old friend by what I believe was divine intervention, and she invited me to her church. The youth group and the pastor poured into me and prayed over me. I began writing songs and poems daily to just make it through school and work. I could not wait to get to the church three and four times a week. I chose to focus on Jesus. For the first time in my teen years, I was completely God dependent doing faith prompted work without a need or desire to pursue boys or things that would pull me away from who God designed me to be. I believed in the better life, the future, the hope, that He promises in Jeremiah 29:11. I believed that nobody on this Earth had any power to take this away from me or decide for me my future. It was then that I wrote this poem: "I Won't"

"I won't change who I am for what
someone wants me to be,
Unless I know its Jesus, the one I'll someday see.
I won't change what I feel for others to agree,
Unless I'm sharing truth about the
man who died for me.
I won't walk the devil's direction to
be accepted by my friends,

I want to be like Jesus though He
was alone He never sinned.
I won't say I think I'm perfect, tho'
some say I think I am,
The world can say whatever, but there's
just one Precious Perfect Lamb.
I won't talk the talk if I know it is a lie
People don't understand how hard us Christians try
I won't walk the walk if I feel I'll one day stray,
But for those who walk with this ungodly
world will get their's Judgement Day.
I won't sing the profanity of my
foes I often hear them sing
Being like everyone else just is not my thing
I won't take my mountains for granted
or dwell on valleys sorrow
I'll just be thankful I have God to
get me through tomorrow.
I won't boast on my success, and leave
my problems in His Hand,
After all He knows it all, He's Creator of this land.
Just lift your eyes to Jesus, He'll never leave your side
He knows how you truly feel so do not try and hide.
I won't blame the ones around me, I
make mistakes on my own.
When you get the urge to point, think what Jesus said,
"Thou who is without sin cast the first stone". Look to
God for strength and comfort when you feel alone
He's the Master and the Healer because
we can't make it on our own.

"There is a time for everything,
and a season for every activity under the heavens..."
Ecclesiastes 3

God's timing is perfect. Feeling the love of Jesus Christ was a real need in my life and He answered. I put my dependence on God and my focus on my home in Heaven rather than my home on Earth. I had to. Every day I would come home from school, a piece of our furniture, a piece of our life, would be gone. My mom was selling our belongings off one by one. The work hours at Kmart were tough. It was becoming frequent that we were out of bread and toilet paper. I got off work sometimes around midnight and had to be up at 6 for school. I was so tired. I had no idea that the changing day of my life was quickly approaching. I came home from school to take a nap before my work shift started. I think it was one of the times in my life where a nap was as valuable as winning the lottery. I needed sleep. I got home and went straight to bed. I was asleep for nearly an hour when my mom walked into my room with a complete stranger. This stranger was a haggard looking woman that I had never seen before. My mom had a strange smile on her face...the kind of look that people make when they are fighting back their real emotions and putting a smile over it. I never want to see it again. She said, "Keri, get up. This lady is here to get the bed. She paid me money so now it's hers." I remember thinking, "My bed is gone? She sold my bed? I have to sleep on the floor? How can this be my life?"

The remaining days of my senior year of high school were spent coming home to an empty townhouse, no food, no furniture, no family. Yet, I believed Luke 12:31, that He will supply my needs, and that the Lord designed a better life for me (Jeremiah 29:11). All I needed to do was take the right steps to find it.

Look In The Book

When I was little, we sang a song in junior choir called "Look in the Book". The words said, "Look in the book for the answers to all the questions that are puzzling you". Seemed pretty simple to me. I had all of these questions so I looked to God's word for the answers. The Lord blessed me with opportunities to share my Faith despite the circumstances in my family.

One day I came home and found my mom really upset. "Momma, why are you crying?" She replied, "Because we can not afford for you to go to college. I don't know what you are going to do!" I looked at her and I said, "Momma, scripture tells us that all things are possible in the Lord. If it is God's design for me to go to college, then I will." I turned over every stone to find financial aid and scholarships. I kept a 4.0 through my entire senior year and that by itself was a real miracle from God. I received scholarships to Mississippi State University that covered part of my tuition and books.

A few months before I left for college, I met a guy that went to MSU through a fellow youth group member at church. I knew that he was not a Christian. I knew that I should not date him because our beliefs were not the same. I knew better than God what was good for me. I allowed my fear of being alone, my fear of not having money, my fear of not feeling valued, my fear of not having a safe place to fall, move me from my faith in what the Lord promised me in Jeremiah 29:11 to decisions motivated by fear. I quickly stepped away from the path designed by God to pursue the path designed by Keri. The relationship was not healthy. It cost me friendships, but I put a smile on quite well in front of my family. I experienced constant anxiety over trying to make my life look "together" when it was really falling apart. The people that loved me, like my college roommate Karen, knew that he was not God's best for me. I stayed in the relationship because I believed a series of lies the enemy used to tackle me with on a daily basis. "Keri, no one else will put up with your family circumstances. You are not very pretty so finding someone else as good as him will be really tough. He provides for you and you can not make it financially without him. This is as good as it will get for you. You can not let your other friends get hitched before you because you have been dating this guy way longer". Do NOT miss this point: the greater things that the Lord has promised to provide us over and over through His Word - in John 1, Genesis 28, and Isaiah, - can and WILL be instantly diminished when we move away from His plan towards our own. Do not be moved by fear and lies from the enemy. Nothing is fruitful outside the path He designs for us.

John 15 says, "I am the true vine, and my Father is the gardener. [2] He cuts off every branch in me that bears no fruit, while every branch that does bear fruit he prunes[a] so that it will be even more fruitful. [3] You are already clean because of the word I have spoken to you. [4] Remain in me, as I also remain in you. No branch can bear fruit by itself; it must remain in the vine. Neither can you bear fruit unless you remain in me.

Keri Ann Unsworth

Keri's Plan: Apart from the Vine

Keri's plan of a few dates turned into almost 7 years, a year and a half of an unhealthy, short, yet abusive marriage, and lifelong consequences. If I would have "looked in the book" for answers and trusted in God's word rather than trying to make up my own rules, then I would have avoided 7 years of pain, confusion, and mediocrity. I settled for less than God's best for me. I will never know what spiritual blessings I diminished that God had waiting for me because I decided to detour. Who did God have for me that I passed by? What experiences did I miss because I was consumed by my own plan?

You may be reading this and asking yourself, "What is the point of sharing this background information?" Keep on reading and you will see that His Grace Abounds and we are not able to out sin His Grace. The entire purpose of this book series is to drive home with practical application the reality that His Grace is infinite and all of us are promised the greater things in His perfect design for our lives. Your past does not determine your future, but you have to take action - get on your knees and repent, believe the promises in His Word, and pursue His Design fearlessly.

Living Apart from the Vine Reaps Eternal Consequences

How severe is it when we step out of God's design? For me, the outcome was total brokenness, on the floor in my college apartment at Clemson University alone, weeping, for hours. The pain of my divorce at the young age of 23 was too much to bear. I came from a very conservative family. There were questions of my faithfulness and fidelity, and I ran from God for several months because facing the opinions of my family, even my own sister, was too much to bear. I took on three jobs, partied every night, and totally lost sight of the person God designed for me to become. I drank my way through a year-long separation from my estranged husband. Despite godly counsel, I began dating and I dropped out of church and partied with people that had no idea that I once pursued a relationship with Jesus. I went to therapy for a year and started to realize that there was a lot about me that needed to change and mature. I learned in therapy that there are generations of infidelity, addiction, and divorce on both sides of my family. I actually believed that I had nothing useful for the Lord and I was not worthy of any other lifestyle than the one I was living. I was covered in sin and the furthest I could ever be from the daughter that God designed.

I went right into another temporary relationship with a very cute baseball coach. This was really no surprise, but I was too covered in sin to have any objectivity about my life and I was too stubborn to listen to counsel. One thing is true for all of us. A life running from God can only last so long. On a rainy night in Central, South Carolina, at my apartment in The Reserves I got on my knees and I begged the Lord for peace, forgiveness, and relief. This is the darkest moment I have ever experienced in my life. My x was working hard to discredit my reputation with the people that I was closest to. He made accusations of infidelity and much worse. I found myself contemplating ending my own life. The pain of my choices and behaviors came pouring down on me like the cold February rain outside my window. I spent so much energy trying to cover up my sin and lifestyle that I had no one to turn to for fear that I would have to confess the reality of the place and position of my heart. I turned off the light in my room and turned up the Dave Matthews Band in hopes to drown out the realness of the broken life I had. I asked the Lord for counsel and He laid my Uncle Jack on my heart. My Uncle Jack and Uncle Frank had been support networks for me, great men of god, great family men, and they believed in me and believed for me through my parents divorce and every obstacle I encountered through those years. I picked up the phone and I called Jack, and the words the Lord gave him were perfect, biblical, full of grace, and they pointed me back to God's Word. Romans 8: 1-2, "Therefore, there is now no condemnation for those who are in Christ Jesus."

I laid all my cards out on the table. I knew the road ahead was going to be hard and difficult, but the hope I found in God's promises that there are greater things available to me moved me forward. The next weekend the Lord sent me a gift in the form of friendship. I got a call from Rachael Wiles who invited me to "get away" and come with her to Charleston to play in a volleyball tournament. She mentioned that the group she plays with loves the Lord and I would not be judged for the circumstances of what I was going through. That Saturday night, I spent hours praying and asking the Lord for peace and clarity about the next stage of my life. I begged God to comfort me and allow me to believe that there is a second chance for my life. After a year of therapy, I saw no way out of an abusive marriage that was not healing. How could it be that I was 22 years old and in this stupid situation? I wiped my tears back and turned over in my sleeping bag. At around 2 A.M., a group of girls invited us to Seacoast Baptist Church in Charleston. For some unknown reason, we felt drawn to this church. I had been away from church for more than a year. I was nervous about going, but I believed I was right where the Lord meant for me to be that morning. We walked into the service and a song by Creed, "Six Feet From the Edge" was playing. They had the lyrics flashing across the screen, and a particular phrase caught my attention, "I thought I found the road to somewhere, Somewhere in His Grace". At this moment, I began to realize that somewhere I had lost sight of the realness of His Grace. I started immediately thinking about the Cross and the sin that Jesus covered for me. As I looked up toward the stage at Seacoast Baptist Church, I started to wonder if maybe God had still had a plan for my future even though I sinned, I settled, and I had totally walked away from the woman He designed me to be. What happened next was absolutely mind blowing. The church usher passed down bulletins or note cards for the sermon to all of us. When one reached me, I felt the presence of God, and I opened up the sermon notes and the title of the sermon was, "Dealing with Divorce"...not "you are damaged..." or "you are worthless" or "you are not worthy"...WOAH!!!

It was that day I realized my sin in entering a marriage that should have never been; yet, still covered by the Cross. Married people need to fight hard and do whatever it takes to stay together. God can heal any marriage. Please do NOT take away from this that I endorse people getting a divorce. This is simply that God was showing me that the Cross covered all of my sin, including my decision to settle and endeavor in a marriage that should have never been. His Grace Abounds above all of our sin and our circumstances. We can not out sin the depth of His Grace. He promises Redemption and He will correct our path. Understand that I kept my wedding ring on, I engaged in counseling with my ex, for an entire year. Divorce is not God's best for us, and I was learning to understand God's word and position on divorce. I begged the Lord for release from my shame and my guilt. You see, the enemy was telling me that I was useless to God because of my bad choices. The enemy pressed on my mind that I was dirty, used, and that no one would find any value in me or certainly in my testimony. But, the Lord used that message, not to condone my decisions and behavior, but to focus me back on His Word and His promises and to uncover the lies the enemy was using to keep me depressed. What kept running through my mind was the favorite verse that I had held onto for 10 years. Jeremiah 29:11, his word promises a "hope and a future. To prosper us and not to harm us". His Word does not change. In Ephesians 3:20, His Word promises us a life beyond what we can hope for or imagine and that is *always* available to us.

Jeremiah 29:11: For I know the plans I have for you," declares the Lord, "PLANS TO PROSPER YOU AND NOT TO HARM YOU, PLANS TO GIVE YOU HOPE AND A FUTURE.

There was hope in Him. There was a second life. Instead of receiving condemnation for my sin, I received an embrace and a hope and a future. I was able to learn biblically what I needed to do moving forward to live under His protection. I started to weep, not just cry, but weep. This was a changing day in my life with a renewed commitment to walk with Jesus no matter what it was going to take. When I returned home, I shared the message and the scriptures with my ex in hopes for his salvation and that He would turn his life around. I shared with him that I have forgiven him and that the Lord has a new design for us regardless of our past. From that weekend on, the Lord has brought blessing after blessing with each step I take in His design for my life.

<u>We Are Made To Worship</u>

Led by His Word, I knew that I needed to find a church to plug in to. I was waiting tables at O'Charley's in Anderson, South Carolina. Some people that I waited on at the restaurant mentioned to me a new church had started meeting at Anderson College (now Anderson University). I shared my story that I was recently divorced and in graduate school at Clemson. I had a bad experience attending a local church in Clemson that really pushed me aside when they found out I was recently divorced at the young age of 23. I was afraid to go back to church. I do not even remember who first invited me to NewSpring, but I do remember as though it were yesterday my friend Rachael had visited there and she promised me, guaranteed me, that I would not feel condemned if I visited. I was skeptical because I grew up Southern Baptist and it was a "non-denominational" church. The body of the church met in the Anderson College auditorium. About 150 people were in attendance. The pastor, Perry Noble, preached from the Bible what scripture defines as God's design for healthy relationships. It was the first of what would become many of the notable relationship series' for men and women, single, divorced, widowed, and married people. How was I raised in church, but clueless that God's word actually provides criteria of God's best for us in a mate? And my parents were no model that I wanted to follow. On that day, I gave the Lord my full commitment to adhere to His Word and not date anyone that did not meet the criteria. What I did not know is that my newfound dependence on God would lead to a very lonely dating life! I was at peace living a God dependent life that began to immediately bring the greater things He promises in His Word! I was surrounded by people that were sold out to a commitment to follow Jesus, rather than just wear a church tattoo. The people at NewSpring were from all walks of life that had amazing stories of healing and deliverance. I could see in the body of Christ at this church the "greater things" alive in the lives of people following Jesus. By His Word, I learned that there were several lies from the enemy I spent years believing that were hindering the growth of my relationship with Jesus. More than anything, I could see living examples of what it means in God's Word to receive Grace.

"But he said to me, "My grace is sufficient for you, for my power is made perfect in weakness. Therefore I will boast all the more gladly about my weaknesses, so that Christ's power may rest on me." 2 Corinthians 12:9

The bondage of lies from the enemy affected my choices in men and friendships. I made a choice to start living with a sole point of reference for the Truth, and that is God's Word. And God's Word tells me that I am a daughter of the King, fearfully and wonderfully made (Psalm 139:14), with a hope and a future (Jeremiah 29:11), able to bear much fruit (John 15:1-2), and called to be a disciple to glorify Him (Acts 17:22-23). All of this brings me to the key messages the Lord has laid on my heart for this first book. A real relationship with Jesus begins when we understand and accept His Grace is a gift. Grace is nothing that we can earn and nothing that we can lose. His design and the greater things He promises are always available to us, but we have to receive it. I share with the ladies that I mentor that THE key to experiencing the joy and peace He promises in His Word is 100% belief that His Grace IS sufficient for you. You are new in Christ. My identity was who I was in Christ Jesus rather than who I was dating, or what I was wearing, or what I was doing… especially doing wrong.

Do You Want the Gift?

"Whatever things you ask in prayer, believing, you will receive" Matthew 21:22

Accepting the gift of His Grace brings freedom from sin, lies and labels, and moves you away from anything that does not move you towards God's design for your life and the rewards that He promises in His

Word. When we have accepted His Grace, repented, and asked for a relationship with Jesus in prayer, then we practice life with belief that we are new in Christ. The real transformation that moves someone from "I am a Christian" into a fruit bearing "Christ like" living vessel begins when their acceptance of His Grace is backed by belief in His promises set out in His Word. Do you want the gift of His Grace? Have you prayed to receive it? Are you studying His Word? Do the steps you are taking coincide with the commands in His Word? If you are still saying the same negative things about yourself and focusing on your past life of mistakes and failures, then you have not accepted His Gift of Grace.

PROCLAIM WITH YOUR VOICE: Say this out loud now and everyday the enemy wants to remind you of your past. "The supernatural power of Jesus Christ lives in me. Proclaim out loud right now, 'I am no longer that person. My past does not and will not define me. I believe God's word and the promises in His Word define me. I am purposed for God's purpose and promised a future of greater things".

"For you were once darkness, but now you are the light in the Lord. Walk as children of light, for the fruit of the Spirit is in all goodness, righteousness, and truth, finding out what is acceptable to the Lord" (Ephesians 5: 8-9).

A Life Acceptable and Pleasing
To the Lord is Possible!

Your new life in the embrace of His Grace is a pursuit of what is acceptable to the Lord. You are now a dear child of God positioned to pursue great things for the Lord equipped by the supernatural power of Jesus Christ that now lives in you. Accepting the Gift of His Grace means that you believe this without conditions.

Say it ALOUD!!!

"Lord, I believe that by Your Gift of Grace alone I am able and equipped to have a life full of purpose. I believe You designed a life specifically for me to bring You glory and build Your Kingdom. I believe that every scenario in my life from birth to this point, no matter how sinful, hurtful, painful, or traumatic, can now bring glory to Your Name and bring others to Jesus. I believe in the power of my own testimony. I believe by the Gift of Your Grace, I am designed with a purpose to overcome the enemy, to defeat any force that hinders the pursuit of YOUR design for my life (Revelation 12:11 "by the blood of the Lamb and the word of our testimony").

Ladies, it is BIBLICAL AND PROMISED!!!

John 15:11 says, "I have told you this so that my joy may be in you and that your joy may be complete".

Deuteronomy 16:15 says, "For the Lord your God will bless you in all your harvest and the work of your hands, and your joy will be complete".

Lord, I believe the Gift of Your Grace brings spiritual fulfillment designed just for me. Ladies, now you are believing for the experience of a greater life, which builds a heart that longs to know Him and a heart that wants to spend time in His Word to gain knowledge about what is acceptable and pleasing to Him. When we really believe in and accept the unconditional Gift of His Grace, we are free to begin experiencing divine intercession in our lives. The work that God can do through you when you believe is incomprehensible, and so far beyond what our human ability even allows us to conceive.

Ephesians 3:20, "Now to him who is able to do immeasurably more than all we ask or imagine, according to his power that is at work within us."

Walking In Grace Filled Shoes

Ephesians 5: 8-9 says, "For you were once darkness, but now you are the light in the Lord. Walk as children of light, for the fruit of the Spirit is in all goodness, righteousness, and truth), finding out what is acceptable to the Lord."

At this point in the journey, its 2002 and I am actively worshipping at NewSpring Church. I am a 23-year-old divorcee attending graduate school at Clemson University pursuing a Master of Arts degree in Professional Communication. I have a great group of friends that are following Jesus. I believe in the infiniteness of His Grace and the second will He has designed for my life. I am lonely, but excited about the future ahead of me. I was going through the daily motions and being diligent in my jobs and my school work. I was so busy checking off the boxes to stay sane that I had no idea that a church sermon was about to transform my life. I really do not recall the exact title of the series, but it was Perry Noble's very first series on relationships. How could this be? I have been in church all my life, yet had no idea that the Lord has laid out His design for healthy relationships and marriage with specific scripture. I slowly began to realize that I had to make major changes in my behavior and the choices I was making in my dating life and social life in order for me to experience God's best for me. In one sermon, the Lord embraced me, and the voice of the Holy Spirit so eloquently and benevolently whispered to me, "Keri, you are a daughter of the King. You are valuable. You matter. You can live a wholesome life because the same power that lives in me is alive in you. You are not that person anymore. You can begin again in me and experience great rewards. You have a purpose that I formed in you before your parents even knew you!" I realized that the beliefs I had about myself and the labels that had been thrown at me were lies that do not align with what God's promises are for me according to His Word. It is spiritually impossible for me to practice being a Christian and walk in the light if I am holding on and held back by the mistakes of my past and the poor behavior of my previous lifestyle. Real belief comes from practicing and proclaiming that you are NOT THAT PERSON ANYMORE! You are just as equipped as anyone to do whatever He sets before you.

How do I Get There? Cutting off the crisis of belief!

Every lady wants to know the answer to "How do I get there from here?" The answer is by putting on your Grace filled shoes and start walking!

In My Grace Filled Shoes, Lord, Here I Am!

The first step of walking in the light is saying "*Lord, Here I Am*." How do we know this? Just take a look at the life of Abraham in the book of Genesis. Read Genesis 22.

Genesis 22: 1
Some time later God tested Abraham. He said to him, "Abraham!" "Here I am," he (Abraham) replied.

Many of God's best examples for leaders who walked with fully surrendered commitment to His plan are in the Old Testament in the book of Genesis. The story of Abraham is an excellent picture of an obedient faith driven walk that was pleasing and acceptable to the Lord. In Genesis, scripture points out that Abraham was blessed in many aspects of life. He was anointed by God to be the father of many generations. Abraham's faith impacted people and cities around him. But, the clearest picture of faith prompted obedience that God requires us to imitate is Abraham's action to sacrifice his son Isaac. In Abraham's life, God tested his faith many times.

When God called Abraham (then Abram) to Canaan, he had to pack up and leave everything behind. He had no idea what the outcome would be. All he knew is that he was called by God to move. During the years of settling in Canaan, the Lord affirmed several promises to Abram and changed his name to "Abraham" with the promise that he would be a father to many nations. The Lord promised Abraham that he would give him another son that would be born when Abraham was more than 90 years old. God fulfilled that promise too and along came Isaac. Abraham walked in faith and was known as a peacemaker. Abraham was called by God again to sacrifice his son Isaac on Mount Moriah. Abraham climbed up the mountain in obedience to reach the top as called by God. Can you imagine Abraham knowing that at the top he was called by God to give up, kill, sacrifice his son because God commanded him to do so? Yet, he climbed and continued towards the place God called him to. At the last moment in the highest exhibition of sacrifice, the Lord called Abraham to move his hand and He presented a ram in the bushes for Abraham to sacrifice in Isaac's place. So again, the Lord answered with favor on Abraham because of his faithful obedience.

All Abraham did is say to the Lord, "Here I Am" and walk towards where the Lord called him. The pattern of faith in Abraham's life was consistent even when the circumstances did not make sense. Standing before the Lord with a "Here I Am!" sincerely sold out to self with outstretched arms is what the Lord commands us to do and he used Abraham to show us how to do it. None of us know where our walk with Jesus is going to lead us, but Abraham like faith requires that we believe for the reward and not focus on or be led by fear of the outcome.

We probably do not think that beginning this major life changing walk could be as simple as saying, 'Lord, Here I Am!', but Abraham's life is proof! Saying "Here I Am" and following through on what He says for us to do in our walk is really all it takes. If you look at Abraham's life, imagine had he not answered the Lord, the blessings, favor from the Lord, and impacting generations that would not have taken place. Most of us probably do not really know what we would do if the Lord commanded us to sacrifice our child or someone we love. Ladies, do not miss this! The condition of Abraham's commitment to sacrifice Isaac is exactly where we need to be spiritually.

The Lord shows us through the life and faith of Abraham that being fully surrendered means that we walk in His Word and by His Word above everything that our own desires. Can you imagine how Abraham must have felt? Abraham probably looked around and saw other animals that could be sacrificed, but the important characteristic we learn from his faith is that Abraham did not question God. Abraham did not try to make sense out of the circumstances. He just kept walking to the place of sacrifice believing in God's promise of redemption.

Most of us would question God and run out of patience. We would take over control and start trying to make things happen on our own. But Abraham knew the Lord would fulfill His promise. Abraham knew that reaching the top without God's plan is failure. Abraham believed that abundance by the promises from God would be provided and the only rewards worth living for are the eternal rewards from God. We would probably go and hide if God asked us to do something this crazy. The Lord shows us in Abraham's life that truly walking with Jesus in the light has to come without conditions, with a simple, 'Here I am" Lord,' just like Abraham. The spiritual and financial outcomes of Abraham's faith impacted everyone around him for the glory of the Lord. You see Abraham did not sit around when the Lord commanded him to sacrifice Isaac. He did not travel to a nearby city and seek counsel. He did not hold a committee meeting and get others opinions. He simply spent time with Lord, surrendered self, and moved forward to the next step and prepared the sacrifice with surrendered belief that the Lord would answer. Abraham was always moving in the direction of the image of God. That is why it is called a "walk" – because the Lord requires us to be constantly stepping out of our own character to become more like the character of God. And the reason the Lord provides us His word is for us to see real pictures of His faithfulness and to exemplify the multitude of spiritual blessings that result when we follow Him without questioning. One step at a time, we walk towards God's design for us. The steps that we take are only known by the power of His Word.

Psalm 119:105 "Your word is a lamp to my feet and a light for my path"

PRAYER:
Heavenly Father, Faithful God, my flesh is so weak and my mind often fights against what I know you have commanded me to do for your glory. In the past I have not been willing to give up things that are important to me but are clearly not part of your design for my life, but I am asking that you give me the right heart for obedience, the courage to obey, no matter the circumstances. Lord, I say to you, "Here I Am". Please design my life to meet your purposes and not my own. Please give me the patience to wait to hear from you and give me the commitment to learn and remain in Your Word so I can recognize when Satan is moving me from faith to fear. Give me strength to surrender everything and give me the discernment to

know with clarity what opportunities are from you, and to imitate you as your word transforms me into the image of Jesus.

Walking in Grace Filled Shoes Brings Rewards

Genesis 22:13
Abraham looked up and there in a thicket he saw a ram caught by its horns. He went over and took the ram and sacrificed it as a burnt offering instead of his son.

Ladies, imagine the moment when Abraham reached the top of the mountain and placed his son on the altar. The emotional distress he must have experienced as he raised his hands up in motion to slay his son was more than any of us can comprehend. Abraham was serious about his commitment to obeying God's commands. Abraham in the final moments did not know that the Lord had a ram in the bush. Do you want God's best for you? Do you want to be blessed in all things the way the Lord blessed Abraham? God's best for you is not attainable unless we follow His commands with a heart that loves Him and fears Him. God has designed a ram in the bush experience for us all! Women who have the fear and love and reverence for the Lord receive God's love and many spiritual rewards. The secret of experiencing God like Abraham did rests in the position of our heart. God wants our hearts to be all for Him so that He can transform us and reward us. Obedience in scripture always comes with rewards. The leaders appointed by God followed Him and

Kept His commands even when they could not see the rewards their commitment would bring.

The Lord reinforces this through scripture. In Hebrews 11:6 he says, "⁶ And without faith it is impossible to please God, because anyone who comes to him must believe that he exists and that he rewards those who earnestly seek him." The Lord demonstrates in verse 22 that Abraham did not withhold even his son from the Lord. The Lord wants us to have hearts that will not hold back from what He asks us to do.

Ladies, we have to be in awe of His greatness and believe that He is the one true God and that He is GOOD! Keeping His commands is a spiritual void when we do not obey with love in our hearts and a fear of the Lord. The ram in the bush experiences in Abraham's life show us that all that matters to God is the relationship that we have with Him. He sees what motivates our obedience. He sees the position of our hearts. He wants us to believe in the rewards that He has designed for each of us, but more than anything, He wants to see that our obedience is an outcome of our love and fear of Him. Fearing the Lord comes from faith and belief that the pursuit of a relationship with God and keeping His commands is the eternal adventure that supersedes everything else we set out to do.

Many of us may be thinking, "Why would a sweet loving God that is good ask Abraham to sacrifice his son?" Ladies, do NOT miss this!!! Abraham's belief that the Lord is good carried him through the toughest circumstances that any parent could ever face. God called him to climb up a mountain and sacrifice his son. But

Abraham trusted in the goodness of the Lord and followed through even when he could not see or understand God's plan to use him as a vehicle to build a legacy of faith in God that would transcend generations. "He's not safe, but he's good (referring to Aslan, the Lion, in The Lion, the Witch and the Wardrobe)".

In our relationship with God, it is spiritually impossible to love Him with the strength to keep His commands if our hearts are not trusting and believing in his goodness. Do you think Abraham would have had the strength to sacrifice Isaac if he did not believe any good would come out of it? The Lord is going to test our faith just like he did Abraham. He is going to know if we love him based on how willing we are to not withhold from him anything that he commands us to let go of.

Ladies, we must always know that God is good and our obedience to whatever He calls us to do will be followed by a ram in the bush. God wants our hearts to be consumed with a love for Him and our purpose to be for Him. He wants our obedience to come by gospel driven belief that God's best for us is real and good!

Okay, so how does this apply in your life today? I am living proof that the surest way to begin seeing God transform your life is by simply asking God, "Lord, identify for me the areas in my life that need to be surrendered to you so that you will increase and I will decrease and the plans You have for me prevail and my plans for me will die." By fervent prayer and really asking God to show me, He revealed in my walk that I needed to dress differently. If I wanted a godly man that would love my inside, then I needed to stop dressing with a focus on my outside.

The Lord showed me that I needed to spend time alone with Him and with people that really know Him. My sphere of influence went from downtown Tiger Town Tavern shooting pool and playing Photo Hunt to coffee at Starbucks with groups of wiser women that were where I desired to be. God started to show me what His Word says rather than what our culture says. Like, our culture says, "If it makes you happy, then it can not be that bad" but scripture tells us that our joy and our hope are in Jesus Christ and not temporary experiences like hooking up with boys and drinking.

John 15:11
These things I have spoken to you, that my joy may be in you, and that your joy may be full

PRAYER DIRECTION:
Ask the Lord to position your heart to fear Him and increase your belief that He is good even when the circumstances and what He asks of us do not make sense. Pray that God will give you the right heart for Him and that your obedience would be motivated purely out of love for God and your desire to experience His faithfulness.

What Comes Next is According to Your Faith

Once we accept the Gift of His Grace and we start our walk with Christ, we need the supernatural power that Jesus promises to us in His Word to be alive in our lives.

Matthew 9:29 says, "According to your faith it will be done to you." (NIV)

Matthew 17:20

[20] He replied, "Because you have so little faith. Truly I tell you, if you have faith as small as a mustard seed, you can say to this mountain, 'Move from here to there,' and it will move. Nothing will be impossible for you."

How many times have things happened in our lives where we knew we needed supernatural power? What many of us do not realize is that in Christ, we have supernatural power available to us by the power of the Holy Spirit. And those of us who "know" it, or "see it" may not really "believe" it. But most of us can think of circumstances that have unfolded in our lives as we follow Jesus that are impossible to explain. Our human ability on our own is powerless.

In John 15:5,

God's Word promises, [5] "I am the vine; you are the branches. If you remain in me and I in you, you will bear much fruit; apart from me you can do nothing. [6] If you do not remain in me, you are like a branch that is thrown away and withers; such branches are picked up, thrown into the fire and burned. [7] If you remain in me and my words remain in you, ask whatever you wish, and it will be done for you. [8] This is to my Father's glory, that you bear much fruit, showing yourselves to be my disciples."

Deuteronomy 5:33

Walk in obedience to all that the LORD your God has commanded you, so that you may live and prosper and prolong your days in the land that you will possess.

Robert Morris tells us in his book "The Blessed Life" that evidence of the Holy Spirit in your life creates days "filled with divine coincidences and heavenly meaning" (28 Morris The Blessed Life). He also says that people who follow and sell out to God's design for their life experience joy and completeness that billionaires envy. When we commit to "remain" in Him as he commands in John 15, things get very tough.

So, how do we hold on for the rewards He promises in His Word and stay focused on what He has called us to in order to experience a life rich in joy and completeness? Maybe for you it is waiting for God's best for you in a spouse. For others it may be deliverance from addiction or abuse. For some, its release from being "religious" and getting into a "relationship" with Jesus Christ. Many people just struggle day to day being content with their circumstances. Some of us have faith and trust issues. And others of us want to control everything! So, what can you do to step out of your "normal" and move towards God's plan for "supernatural"?

I believe, based on His Supernatural Presence in my life, that at least four core areas of our lives need to experience transformation.

Four areas that have to experience transformation as we move to the next level:
1. Spiritual
2. Financial
3. Physical
4. Social/Relational

1. The Spiritual Area Of Our Life

#1 "He must become greater"

John 3:30 *"He must become greater; I must become less."*
First, following God's Word in our walk is not optional. I spend time with ladies every day that often ask me, "Why did God bring this terrible man into my life? What is God trying to teach me? Why am I suffering? Why would a loving God do this to me?" I can tell you that 100% of people that are experiencing regret, confusion, anxiety and a lack of control are not staying focused on asking God to become greater and they are probably struggling practicing belief that He has a ram in the bush just for them.

A lot of times this happens because at the end of the day the way we are living is not in alignment with belief that God's word is true. So, spiritual growth begins by believing that the Bible is a book of Truth. It is spiritually impossible to walk in grace filled shoes without believing that God's Word is 100% a book of Truth. When we accept the Gift of His Grace, it is with a heart that believes His Word is True and that is how we accept the gift of His Grace as "sufficient" for us.

If we accept this, and believe His Word is true, then we know that God is good and His promises are real. As I point ladies back to God's word, I ask them questions about their circumstances. For example, how did you meet the "terrible" guy that is cheating on you? Never have I ever had a lady respond with an answer that aligned with what God promises in His word. Simply put, every time a woman lands in an unhealthy relationship, it was usually born out of fear, insecurity, and full of a "me" or "right now" focus rather than "Jesus" and time in "His Word". When we practice God's Word, such as "He must increase, I must decrease" His Arms charge over us and lead us to healthier directions that bring eternal rewards (Psalm 91).

I was meeting one night with one of the girls I mentor. We had established a biblical plan for her life with Jesus centered goals. Two weeks into the plan, she fell away for a few days. I know that typically when my girls disappear or fall off the radar it is usually because of a poor decision or conviction or both. Sure enough, she reached out to me and asked to have coffee. She said, "I have some things I need to talk to you about". And of course, "there is no condemnation for those in Christ Jesus" Romans 8:1 - so full of grace and mercy I showed up! She confessed that she had been seeing and spending time with a partner that she knew was toxic for her, but because she was lonely, fearful, tired, and needing her ego stroked in a moment of weakness she re-opened the gates to this person.

The Lord whispered to me, "Keri, just listen. As she shares with you I am working on her". When she finished sharing, I wrote down to remind her what her main biblical goal was – which at this time was to do everything necessary to follow Jesus and parent her 4 year old daughter. And this is what the Lord put on my heart to say, "Do you believe these behaviors align with God's word and His plan for your future? Do you believe that this investment of time in this toxic person is worth you forfeiting the abundance promised to you in Jeremiah 29:11? Are you really going to trade God's mercy, favor, and completeness of joy for instant gratification that is temporary and unfulfilling, not to mention abusive and devoid of Jesus? I told her that it is spiritually impossible to walk in the light and be comfortable with behaviors that move you in an opposite direction. Then I asked her, "Do you know what God's word says about a lukewarm walk? He says in Revelation 3:16, "So, because you are lukewarm--neither hot nor cold--I am about to spit you out of my mouth." This behavior reflects a lukewarm heart. Is that the direction you want to go?" When I got up from the table, the Lord called me to pray over her. I put my hand on her head and I prayed, "Heavenly Father, whatever this fleshly temptation is I break it off in the name of Jesus. I claim the victory for this girl over this desire that she has that moves her away from your plan and the future you have for her. I pray in the name of Jesus that these feelings and desires will completely dissolve and in the name of Jesus I claim the victory right now". I hugged her and walked away. I am sure she was thinking that I am some crazy woman. The next morning at 8 A.M. I got a phone call from her. "Keri, what did you do to me last night? Whatever that prayer was, whatever you did and said, I woke up this morning and I am not able to explain it, but I am breaking off this relationship and I see so clearly that this needs to happen and will. I just wanted you to know that God answered! I am comforted and at peace and I can not even explain it!" Ladies, the power of Christ in us really IS supernatural! Stop believing you can't, because HE can create amazing change in us that transforms us when we seek Him with all of our heart, soul, mind and strength! We ARE the light! We know this by His Word:

> [5] This is the message we have heard from him and declare to you: God is light; in him there is no darkness at all. [6] If we claim to have fellowship with him and yet walk in the darkness, we lie and do not live out the truth. [7] But if we walk in the light, as he is in the light, we have fellowship with one another, and the blood of Jesus, his Son, purifies us from all[b] sin.
> [8] If we claim to be without sin, we deceive ourselves and the truth is not in us. [9] If we confess our sins, he is faithful and just and will forgive us our sins and purify us from all unrighteousness. [10] If we claim we have not sinned, we make him out to be a liar and his word is not in us. Ladies, let His Word guide your decisions as you walk in the light.

His Word can not fail!!

Luke 1:37
"For nothing in God's Word will ever fail"

#2 Daily evaluation of our spiritual condition

Second, we have to daily measure where we are spiritually. The second element to walking in grace filled shoes spiritually is that we constantly have to evaluate the hidden place of our hearts...our attention to prayer and ministry of the word.

Acts 6:4 says,
"And we will give our attention to prayer
and the ministry of the word."

Scripture Reading: Luke 10:38-42 with key verses: 10:41, 42
Deuteronomy 5:29 that tells us the Lord's commands are to rest in our hearts. In Acts 6:4 God's Word commands us to give attention to prayer and the ministry of the word. Through the life of Abraham we learn that obedience that is pleasing to the Lord comes from a heart that loves God and fears Him. So many of us want to have the right heart and experience God's best for our lives, but moving spiritually to the next level in obedience to God can be intimidating and hard to see. In the story of Mary and Martha in Luke 10:38-42, God's Word gives us a clear picture of what is acceptable to Him. Godly women are characterized by sacrifice, listening to Jesus and hearing His Words, and being devoted to the better part, which is hearing from Jesus by His Word and trusting in His Will for our lives.

What does the Lord point to in verse 38 that shows us the position of Martha's heart? "As Jesus and his disciples were on their way, he came to a village where a woman named Martha _____ her home to him." We see in verse 38 that Martha opens her home to Jesus and the disciples. Wow! What a sacrifice! This was no easy task but Martha had a heart for serving and giving to others. Martha accepts service to Jesus with all of her heart without anticipating what she would receive or what the outcome would be. Martha made herself available to Jesus without conditions and it was very hard work! We are called to be sacrificial women of God and work hard to make ourselves available to him physically and spiritually. Mary died to her reputation while Martha was busy protecting hers.

Spiritual growth is an outcome of hearing from Jesus and His Word. Look at verse 39. "She had a sister called Mary, who _____ at the Lord's feet _____ to what he said." Ladies, DO NOT MISS THIS!!! (READ ALOUD THROUGH verse 42).

> [38] As Jesus and his disciples were on their way, he came to a village where a woman named Martha opened her home to him. [39] She had a sister called Mary, who sat at the Lord's feet listening to what he said. [40] But Martha was distracted by all the preparations that had to be made. She came to him and asked, "Lord, don't you care that my sister has left me to do the work by myself? Tell her to help me!" [41] "Martha, Martha," the Lord answered, "you are worried and upset about many things, [42] but few

Keri Ann Unsworth

things are needed—or indeed only one.[a] Mary has chosen what is better, and it will not be taken away from her."

While Martha was busy doing service oriented things that were good, acceptable and applauded by men, Mary was sitting at the feet of Jesus absorbing his words into her heart. Ladies, so many of us are Martha. We are so busy doing good things and good purposed work that we are not abiding at his feet and listening to His words. Ladies, this is SO critical!! Women are masters at telling other women who they should be, where they should be, what they should be, etc. Our point of reference and our knee bows to one GOD and THAT is where our steps are ordered – at the throne of Jesus by the power of His Word! It is spiritually impossible – IMPOSSIBLE – to walk in the light without time on your knees in His Word! All of us can be great producers of great work, but if it is not God's work and His Purpose it is NOT eternal and void of completeness of joy. Jesus promises in verse 42 that all we need is the better part, which is the time in His Word hearing from Him. Women that have a heart for God are never too busy to sit down with His Word with ears to hear.

The hidden person of our hearts understands that His words are the only lasting reference for our lives that point us back to the Kingdom of God. Matthew 6:33, "But seek _____ his kingdom and his righteousness, and all these things will be given to you as well." The hidden person of the heart seeks Him first. His word begins our work. His word begins our day. His commands drive our lifestyles. His Kingdom is our everything. Acts 6:4 says, "And we will give our attention to prayer and the ministry of the word." Our hearts have to be positioned towards God's priority for our life, which begins at his feet and in His word. The "better part" is Jesus's promise that the word He puts in our hearts can not be taken away. The only thing that is permanent, fulfilling, and eternal for the direction of our lives is the time we spend hearing from Him and applying His word.

It is impossible to take the right steps without hearing from the Lord by His Word and prayer that the order set before us is from Him and not from us. Leaders like Abraham and Mary in the bible knew the intimate God of the Living without applause. For many of us, this can be physical, social, and / or financial distractions.

Psalm 91: 1-2
"Whoever dwells in the shelter of the Most High
will rest in the shadow of the Almighty.[a]
2 I will say of the Lord, "HE IS MY REFUGE AND
MY FORTRESS, MY GOD, IN WHOM I TRUST."

How can we do this? If you ask yourself this question prior to any action or major decision – "Does Jesus increase and myself decrease?" John 3:30. He will answer and you will be protected and empowered. At the end of the day, Jesus has to be ENOUGH! Regardless of the circumstances, conditions, emotions.

Spiritual Evaluation Practice:

What are the things that you need to abandon or minimize so that He can increase in your life? Have you put yourself in positions to serve others without setting your heart right before the Lord? What are some changes that you can make so that you are in His Word more and actively hearing from God?

#3 Believe!

Third, our actions must demonstrate belief. It is spiritually impossible to walk in the light without belief. Do you believe that He is the "author and finisher and perfecter of our faith?" Hebrews 12:1-3.

To follow His commands we must have Faith. The story of how Jesus healed the demon possessed boy in Matthew 17 is a powerful demonstration directly from Jesus that is there for us to look to when we need to feel the presence and power of Jesus. His command to us is to just have faith the size of a mustard seed.

It IS that simple! That is all it takes! I believe that many women are holding back in their lives because they think they have to check off all of the boxes like good service in the church, time with children, cooking dinner, and mapping through that cookie cutter life in order to receive this kind of a miracle from Jesus in their life. His word shows us that this way of thinking could not be more wrong. All it takes is "faith the size of a mustard seed".

Have you ever held a mustard seed in your hand? When Jesus tells us that is all it takes, then we are commanded to believe the gospel and use that gospel to drive our lives. Ladies, do NOT miss this! Jesus said just the grain of a mustard seed. He did not give a list of things we need to achieve, or who we need to know, or what others need to say about us. He says, just step out in faith. He qualifies us for faith by His grace. When we accept His grace and recognize the opportunity to receive the power of Jesus to work through us the guilt, shame, mistakes from our past are dissolved and we experience a joy and freedom that attracts others to us. The power of faith prompted action is infinite. There is no performance, position, or achievement required, just belief in His Word and promises.

Take a step back from your life and look at some of your most recent decisions. Did you spend more time discussing with others your options than you did asking the Lord for guidance? Have you spent more time on social media than you have in His Word? Have you complained more about your spouse than you have on your knees praying for him or her? If we really BELIEVE His Word is true, then we get on our knees and read what He says the point of Truth should be for our lives. *"I am the God of Abraham, the God of Isaac, and the God of Jacob'[a]? He is not the God of the dead but of the living." Matthew 22:32.* When our obedience is motivated by our belief that He is the God of the Living, then our light shines as we are alive in Christ . The ram, the sacrifice, the story of Abraham and Isaac is the essence of the faith prompted work and action that we are commanded to live out in our lives.

Keri Ann Unsworth

The power of others seeing our faith, if you look at how Abraham's faith when he surrendered his son Isaac and how it impacted generations and people simply believed because of his faith in God's plan, is the core of walking in the light and imitating Him. In 1 John 1, scripture focuses again on what has been seen and heard and the people are proclaiming it. When others see us make decisions in faith by God's calling and His word about our families, our jobs, our relationships, our children, our finances, our giving, they are impacted and their belief grows. When we share the outcomes of our prayer, time in His word, as we move with faith prompted steps, the Lord builds stories in us that we are commanded to proclaim and reinforce that He is faithful and His word is true.

In November of 2013 I miscarried what would have been our second child. This is my Facebook post. "After a little over 6 weeks, Jon and I had to let go of a pregnancy that was not in God's timing. God is good and God is faithful! I was supposed to be on the road to Cincinatti yesterday but because the weather was bad I prayed and believed it better to leave on Tuesday. How GOOD is God that I experienced this miscarriage at home and not on the road. THANK YOU JESUS! I prayed Sunday night that if this trip was not God's best for our family, that He would make it known. Wasn't expecting that kind of answer but I praise the Lord and I am thankful that God showed mercy and His Love. My church family surrounded me today both physically and spiritually and I am SUCH a blessed woman! Ever so thankful for my 4 year old who is an absolute perfection of God's image! The expansion of our family will happen by God's design. God knows my heart and that if it is not from Him and not His Plan then we don't want it! Thank you Jesus!" I had physical challenges that were extremely painful. I began begging God for mercy on my body and to move me through this physically and spiritually with His Supernatural Power. My husband prayed over me as well. My spiritual condition was never compromised, yet strengthened by complete reliance on Him. Isn't it amazing how when our bodies weaken and we are forced to recognize we are totally powerless in our flesh that we quickly look up for help from the Lord. My eyes stayed focused on God's plan, but not just for me, but for everyone in my sphere of influence that was engaged with this traumatic experience. By His Amazing Grace and Supernatural Spirit, I received an unbelievable peace that surpasses all understanding. He raised me up in less than three days I was back at my company working and serving my family with joy and excitement for the future. I literally felt that God was carrying me and my family. When I was sitting in the doctor's office at the beginning of this, I immediately turned on my praise music on my phone. You see, the night before this happened I was leading our home group on having Abraham like faith regardless of how circumstances change. I pleaded with them to believe that God always has a ram in the bush if we trust Him and stay out of His Way. I used my own "seed" that God had so miraculously planted in my womb as an example of believing prayer. Jon and I had prayed for four years for this baby. I had NO idea that I would experience this loss the next morning. Yes, a true test of our family's faith and everyone seemed to be watching. From the very first spot of blood, I gave it over to Jesus. I sang with my arms raised in the dr.'s office, I thanked Him, I praised Him for the amazing family that I have. And I did not stop. Yes, I cried. I grieved A LOT. Alone mostly. But I was not alone. The presence of a Holy God surrounded me so strongly and His Voice kept whispering to me to just trust in His Timing and His Plan. I asked God to help my life and this experience to bring Him Glory. I never questioned "Why" and I did not give any time to "self pity". Only once did I get angry and ask God, "Why is everything so hard for me?" But God answered and said, "Because you give me glory, you trust in me, and you are my vessel". The next day I was picking up my son from preschool and one of the workers said to me, "I saw your Facebook posts. I hope I can have the kind of faith that you do someday." And I looked her in the eye and I said, "You can. All you have to do is ask and believe." The rest of the week was one of the most fruitful and productive weeks I had over the previous 4 years. God is good. I believe. God is faithful. I believe. His Word is True. I believe. His promises are real. I believe. How beautiful that God could use my loss to bring people closer to Him through my belief. Do you trust Him through every circumstance? Do you believe when it does not make sense? Is it really possible to suffer such tremendous loss and sing praise to Him? Yes! Mark 9:23 tells us that "Everything is possible if you can believe". Believing and walking in faith that God is the God of the Living is a command. Do we really grasp the power of what God lays out in Matthew 22? God is the God of the living.

No other God is before him with a Holy book that has transcended more than 2,000 years. Our obedience has to begin in belief that He is the God of the Living and in Him we all have a hope and a future, for Him to prosper us and not to harm us (Jeremiah 29:11).

2. The Physical Area Of Our Life

1 Corinthians 9:24 says, [24] "Do you not know that in a race all the runners run, but only one gets the prize? Run in such a way as to get the prize."

Have you every really thought about the real meaning of this passage and where your steps are headed? Did you ever realize that scripture provides us a guide that takes us straight towards Jesus? The Lord makes at least three characteristics very clear in scripture about how we are to physically run our race as believers.

1. Our life's purpose is about our Savior and not our SELF!
2. Our belief in our Savior leads to behavior that produces fruit.
3. We move forward towards Christ and never look back (remember Lot's wife)

Physical Transformation:
#1: Our life's purpose is about our Savior and not our SELF!

The ultimate destination that we are called to, designed for, and purposed to reach as believers is eternity with Christ. Our ultimate purpose is to further the gospel and invest in eternal things that are not about the here and now. "I press on toward the goal to win the prize for which God has called me heavenward in Christ Jesus,"

Philippians 3:14. "Therefore, holy brothers and sisters, who share in the heavenly calling, fix your thoughts on Jesus…" Hebrews 3:1 says. Revelation 3:11 says, "I am coming soon. Hold on to what you have, so that no one will take your crown." And again, "12 Fight the good fight of the faith. Take hold of the eternal life to which you were called when you made your good confession in the presence of many witnesses," says 1 Timothy 6:12. Our High Calling is to continually look to Christ and set our "eye upon the mark". If someone were to take a close look at your life, then what do you think your life seems to be about? Think about the conversations you have with people every day. What keeps you awake at night? Is it professional position, frustration with certain people, feeling discontent all the time, not having enough money, not enjoying parenthood, feeling defeated all of the time, etc. What do you think about most often? What do you worry about? What do others see you dealing with in your life? How are you dealing with it?

My personal testimony regarding how I was running my race is convicting and powerful. You see, I was a bit over 30 years old, headed up the corporate ladder in a very glamorous position, and most of my days were spent either frustrated about a co-worker or my boss or mad that I was not getting paid as much as others on my team. When I really began to accept the gift of His Grace in my life and press hard towards Jesus, the Lord completely transformed me on the inside and on the outside.

My Life Is Not About Me - Keri Unsworth's Story

"I was living for me - for my name, my reputation, and my abilities."

I worshiped my corporate identity and income until God used the most valuable things in my life to show me He had a better plan. When life is going your way, it's really easy to think you are responsible. I was the breadwinner in my household and took pride in that. I reached nearly every goal I set for myself. I was well on my way to a Vice-President of Marketing position in the utility industry with a large income. By man's measures, I was living the good life; and my husband and I built a lifestyle committed to that income. I was losing focus on the greatest blessing ever: my family and the daily experiences shared. Attached to my phone, I was consumed with trying to control a corporate environment for my betterment. It was all about me.

I was living for me - for my name, my reputation, and my abilities.

At the age of nine Jesus became my Savior, and knew deep down that I was called to serve others just as Christ did. I just didn't know how or what that meant yet. Somewhere between my parents' divorce, poor influence of my peers, and my own selfish ambition, I lost sight of God's design and purpose for my life and went the other direction. I was living for me - for my name, my reputation, and my abilities.

Then God went to work in my life to clean up my mess. In the summer of 2010, Pastor Perry preached a message making it clear you cannot worship both God and money. I looked at my actions. I was not tithing. God was not first in my finances. And in most cases, I was not even giving Him what was left over because I had very little left after my shopping sprees and egotistical giving to the needy. Nothing I could say or do would justify me continuing down a path that the Lord was commanding me to leave. I knew the fulfillment I was looking for was not in a promotion or a raise, but in accepting the call on my life to follow Him on faith to wherever He was going to send me. I told my husband, and resigned my job that night in 2010. I could not see what was in front of me nor could I really make any logical sense out of the situation, but I knew God commanded me to leave my career and step out in faith.

It was spiritually impossible for me to remain a corporate woman, and be consumed with the attention from men, the power of position, and a corporate identity that was greater in me than my calling to serve my husband and my child. I fought the Lord on my physical and professional for more than a year after I had my son in 2009. I was miserable and I knew every single day that I was designed to do something else with my life. The fruits in my life were producing self-glorification. The substance of my testimony for charitable giving and faith in Christ was completely compromised because the lack of joy and contentment that comes from the Lord was absent and I was clearly running my race "in vain". The first thoughts and part of my day were focused on how to deal with people and my obsession to control the outcomes was all about my human ability, which is powerless when we are apart from God's will. I wrestled every single day in my office. I walked around for months, "Sigh...Ugh! I know that I am designed and called to be doing something else". You see, it made no sense by man's measures as I had the cookie cutter life, nice income, professional glamour, 4 star hotels, and no worries. But I knew at 9 years of age I had a "High Calling". I begged the Lord to answer for me, "God how will you use me if I am not where I am supposed to be...show me where I should go". He WAS answering me every single day and I kept fighting my flesh and my fear. It was like the story of when God kept calling to Samuel (1 Samuel 3) and Samuel did not recognize His voice. When I finally stepped out and fully surrendered in my heart to what I wanted for me (which was comfort and a stable paycheck and nice trips, etc.) ...when I went before the Lord with a pure heart and said, "Speak, Lord, for your servant is listening"...He answered me clearly and I received it immediately.

The Physical Transformation Continued: #2: We do NOT look back! (Remember Lot's wife)

Luke 17:32 "Remember Lot's wife."

To really accept the gift of His Grace and move forward in Grace Filled shoes, we have to move forward with our eyes focused on our Cross given Christ designed identity. Do you remember the story of Lot's wife? Under her husband's leadership and Heavenly angels, she was advised to flee and not look back from where she came. She was warned to not focus on the past life she was leaving. But, before her race was finished, although victory was quite near, she turned around to look at the city and the people she left behind. In Luke, Christ warns us to not forget Lot's wife. You see, Jesus knows how powerful the enemy is when we enter into a relationship with Jesus, the enemy's greatest tool is to remind us and move our focus back to who we used to be. Perhaps when we look back, it demonstrates a longing for that way of life and demonstrates a lack of belief in God's identity for us. This way of thinking and focusing on our past is in opposition to God's plan for your life. The enemy attacked me in 2010 shortly after I obeyed and left my career, I was getting into a cycle of reflection -the job I had, the coworkers I miss, the parties I missed out on, the paycheck, the security, the shopping, the status, etc. I was starting to dissolve the hope, courage, and expectation by allowing my mind to be trapped by thoughts of what I used to be, where I used to work, what I used to do...and had these circumstances not unfolded in our family - I would probably be stuck right there - not moving forward and not experiencing the joy, freedom, and blessings of the present and the future. Suddenly, I got the news that my dad's wife was diagnosed with lung cancer. The Lord has brought before us circumstances that clearly manifest the importance of living for today - and never waste time looking back. Before I got the news about my mom, I picked up Joyce Meyer's book *Never Give Up* that someone gave me as a gift when I left my career. I realized that taking action day by day with God ordained clarity is what brought us to where we were, and getting into any self focus and pity and dwelling on the past and what is no longer - is going to ruin all the progress that we have made and inevitably compromise us reaching the dream God has set before our family. "Remember Lot's wife"...man that is powerful!!! Looking behind us at any time - with any energy - at any moment is destructive. I was starting to give the past too much of my time. I was beginning to really question, Could I really be a godly woman and live without the attention from men and the applause for my work achievements? I was starting to question everything about me and my present life and my future. Lot's wife lost everything when she looked back - and I realize what I am risking by doing the same. "As a man thinks, so is he" Proverbs 23:7. There is no doubt I want to avoid being where I was so I have to stop thinking about who that was - and give energy and thought only to who I am becoming according to God's purpose for our family and my life. God has called me to go forward into a great future. It is promised. Letting go of what lies behind is required. Do not even consider the things of old. Any former thing is not to be thought of. Why look back and get more of what we have had when we can look forward and enjoy things too wonderful for us to even imagine? Here is a snapshot of writing from my blog that season

> : "- and the thing is - that the last three months has been too wonderful for me and my family - far beyond what I could have designed for myself - so why would I even allow myself to compromise going forward? I realize now that

the way we made it to Christmas is by doing - not thinking! Isaiah 43 ' God IS DOING a new thing." Everyday because I AM doing - as HE "IS" doing will equal progress towards the fabulous future He has in store. God IS building me a ministry. God IS bringing me into business ownership. God IS showing favor on our family and our faith in Him. God IS delivering on every promise he has made in His word. And my part is trusting that He IS no matter what I can or can not see...He IS providing for us and leading us in every situation and because we know this we are enabled to believe the best about the days to come.

Prayer:

Lord, please continue to give me strength to work hard, having the mind to work, taking advantage of opportunities, and embracing responsibility in the midst of total uncertainty about the outcomes. Give me undying courage to achieve what you have called me to do for my family and ministry. I pray that I will not give thought to my old failures, my old path, my old life and in every situation give thanks for the future you ARE building in us. I pray that I will not take any action or make any decision that will take me away from the God given ability to enjoy today or the future. I pray that I will not look back but only forward. Please let every step Jon and I take be towards the blessings, that I experience every blessing meant for my family, for my work, for my ministry – that you designed for us to have. I pray that I will never doubt your mercy is far greater than yesterday's mistakes. Thank you for putting this future before me. Please provide our family and our friends the spiritual energy and the strength and the grace of God to help us go forward. I pray that what we "think" is focused on your plan and will, dissolving our own temptations and selfish desires – whether it is material or emotional or physical. More of you God – and less of me.

The Physical Transformation Continued: #3: Our belief in our Savior leads to behavior that produces fruit.

It's now been five years since I've taken those steps to obey God, and it has been an incredibly fulfilling journey. God has so much more planned for my life than I could have ever dreamed of for myself. He has taken my marketing and business skills and used them for his glory. God uses me by His design in multiple unconventional ways that help change lives and grow the kingdom of God every day by ministering to, serving, and supporting others. I was living for me, and now I'm living out my life calling. It's amazing what happens when God commands us to do something and we follow through. He will never lead us astray. He takes us where we are, with what we have, and leads us to where we are supposed to be. We just have to listen and step out in faith. So, the second core characteristic of physical transformation is the manifestation of fruit in our lives. I can tell you that the Lord has done more work in my life and our family in 5 short years than I can even comprehend. Here is a bulleted list of some of the key developments:

- Ended my employment on September 7 of 2010

- and was out the door Monday, September 10, 2010 without a plan, but led by His Spirit with faith and action.

• Within 2 months, I was on board as the Outreach Director for Ripple of One ministries to perform fundraising, discipleship, and whatever God called me to.

• Over the last 5 years more than 50 divine connections and series' of circumstances have helped develop solutions oriented approaches for empowering communities by furthering the gospel through parent/child development, financial wellness, physical wellness, and spiritual wellness.

• God opened a door for me to be a keynote speaker at a major technical college administrative professionals day and I used the opportunity to share my testimony. It was an experience I will never forget.

• Launched "mybestlifenetwork.com" – that somehow God enabled me to fund without a stable paycheck through the marketing company that He birthed. This is the development of a free online vehicle that offers an information network to reach people far from God through our community non-profit organizations, churches, and volunteer work in the areas of generational poverty, abuse and addiction.

• I was no longer a woman after ambition, self-glorification, and position and paychecks. I was only after God's plan for me no matter what that will require or resort to. I became the woman at home cooking and cleaning and praying more even though for years I never believed I was capable of this. I was consumed with serving my God and my family without thinking at all about me. And, I was joyful and content. I was not moved by the thoughts or perspectives of other women, and what they believed I should and could be doing. I looked to the Cross and asked to have whatever God has designed for me above all else. And in my heart I meant it. And in my home you could see that I meant it. I was home more than I was gone. I was with my husband more than I was with others. I was focused on teaching my son rather than depending on daycare and teachers, I recognized this is my primary job. Its so ironic to see this transformation! In 2007, my realtor brought me to the house we are living in. It was above our price range but I fell in love with it immediately. My sweet mother-in-law looked at me and said, "Well, if you buy this house then you will have to keep working!" I remember thinking, "Of course I will be working! That is just who I am! Ambitious and driven and on to VP of Marketing"! But God had a different plan for me.

- Poured into prayer, fasted, and spent a lot of time on my knees begging God for progress and prosperity for my husband. When I quit my job in 2010, I was the breadwinner by a long shot and Jon was not even done with graduate school. We had a HUGE income deficit and nothing but faith and reliance on Jehovah Jireh that God would meet our needs. We surrendered to possibly losing our home, but we expressed to the Lord this desire of our heart, a pure heart, that our home was not an idol but a gift from Him. 5 Years later we are still in the beautiful home God provided, my husband received a new position with greater pay and his Master's Degree within 6 months of praying and asking God to move the mountains in his way. Part of the miracle in this includes his committee chair getting cancer, which definitely delayed the process, and in addition to this obstacle he missed deadlines beyond his control that the graduate school decided to give leniency to. They do not make exceptions, but we believed through it all that God is bigger than these circumstances and redemption was for certain. The graduate school moved his deadline by one week and Jon got the paperwork finished. He got through this and then he received a call that one of his class credits had expired and he would have to requalify for Biochemistry by enrolling in the class, which was not possible as he was working full-time, OR he could study on his own and take the final exam. He was devastated as this seemed an impossible obstacle. I kept saying to him daily, "God is bigger. Do not give up." Jon's favorite verse is 1 Corinthians 9:24 says, [24] "Do you not know that in a race all the runners run, but only one gets the prize? Run in such a way as to get the prize." He kept praying and working and studying. The

Keri Ann Unsworth

day of his exam he arrived home distraught, heartbroken and disappointed. But everyone that had been praying for him had this supernatural peace that this obstacle would move just like all of the others did. I was sitting outside on our patio when his phone voicemail lit up. I looked inside and saw Jon near tears on the couch. I checked the voicemail and it was his instructor calling to congratulate him. He scored above what he needed to receive his course credits. I ran to him with open arms and said, "Honey! You did it! God answered! You passed!" and of course he did not believe me so he listened to the message himself. What an unbelievable journey! The fullness of His Grace and Supernatural blessings made our cup run over!

- We read His Word. We believe what He says. We prayed. We acted. God answered. My husband's spiritual growth and leadership in our family is impossible to describe in words. The greatest supernatural blessing has been to see God's favor on my husband. My husband never questioned even when we were 3 months behind on our mortgage with no extra money in sight. Even when God called me to a writing project for 7 weeks with no income production. He supported me and prayed hard.

- Within 4 years, the Lord took my expertise and has applied it in the non-profit world for Kingdom purpose. I get paid to perform fundraisers, donor development, and events for organizations that further the gospel. I could not have mapped out by the power of my own mind a career that looks like the one God has designed for me. An even greater testament to His Glory and Mighty Hand and love for us is that God has brought in an income through my business that is strong, stable, and allows for me to work from home with flexibility so that I am wife and mom first. A 40-hour week feels like 15. And I am a more productive wife and mother and God enables me to produce more work in less time with more pay. Every day I wake up in awe of Him and what He can do through us.

My husband, before he met Christ, had received three DUI's, had unhealthy relationships that led to permanent consequences, did not bring a lot of honor towards his parents, lacked gratitude, exhibited reckless behavior and was completely living without purpose and believing the Bible was just a book of stories rather than truth. My husband in Christ, is the spiritual and financial leader of our home, an amazing example to our son of honor, respect, work ethic, and integrity. He appreciates his parents and exhibits self-control and discipline in all things. Rather than letting alcohol and bar scenes and the approval of other people drive his desires, He is focused on the calling in his life as a husband and father, and in his career as a Director of Food Service to share what Christ has done for Him and that His love for us is Real and that His Grace covers every one of us. Before Christ, my husband had no desire to be around people that did not drink alcohol. It made him uncomfortable.

Keri Ann Unsworth

But now, my husband enjoys being around people that are where he wants to be spiritually. He desires to live life in community rather than doing life alone. You see, when we fall in love and surrender our lives to the Lord, the spiritual transformation creates an outward change in how we run our race that is very recognizable to all people.

Jon's testimony is one of many that show how the love of Christ changes us into what we never thought we were capable of being. Most of us have experiences where we were led into bad situations that had terrible outcomes that shared one thing in common – a lack of wisdom and self-control. When we enter into a relationship with Christ, what we desire to do and be begins to slowly change. We want to be better and different than who we used to be.

2 Peter 1:5-6 says, "For this very reason, make every effort to add to your faith goodness; and to goodness, knowledge; and knowledge with self-control, and self-control with patient endurance, and patient endurance with godliness." Paul warns us about the dangers of the body. What we feed will grow. What you feed to your eyes, ears, heart, senses, hands, and entire body will either hinder your race or strengthen your pace. Think of a successful athlete such as Michael Phelps. Phelps trains six days a week and exercises five hours a day and swims 50 miles per week. Professionals add that Michael Phelps diet consists of the calories he needs for energy to give his muscles fuel and to recover and repair the muscles. Athletes like Phelps that achieve a great finish share one thing in common…they are incredibly self-denying. Their affection for achieving

their goal far outweighs giving in to temporary desires that will move them off course. In our race to run in grace filled shoes, we are called to position Holy Affection for God above our personal desires and preferences. The dangers of feeding our flesh inevitably slow us down. Our ultimate task day to day, "as we go", is the race to further the gospel. 1 Corinthians 9:23 says, "23 I do all this for the sake of the gospel, that I may share in its blessings." Acts 8:25 says, "After they had further proclaimed the word of the Lord and testified about Jesus, Peter and John returned to Jerusalem, preaching the gospel in many Samaritan villages." 1 Thessalonians 1 so that "your faith in God has become known everywhere". Galatians 2:2 tells us that if we are believers moving towards Jesus Christ, then our actions demonstrate a focus on sharing the gospel. 2" I went in response to a revelation and, meeting privately with those esteemed as leaders, I presented to them the gospel that I preach among the Gentiles. I wanted to be sure I was not running and had not been running my race in vain." As we run, if we are not sharing the message of Jesus Christ and the testimony of His Grace and Work in our lives, then our race is in vain. The training, self-denial, and amazing performances do not count unless our motivation followed by faith prompted action is for the furthering of the gospel.

Do our busy lives really reflect this High Calling?

The physical effort we put into our spiritual condition is key. It is spiritually impossible to think that you love God, and not care or invest in the things that God cares about, which are time with Him and time in His Word.

Keri Ann Unsworth

Many of us struggle to hear from the Lord, but all of us want to receive and be moved by the power of Jesus in our lives. But how many of us are really putting aside the things that keep us busy and consumed to take time out and honor Him by giving him the first of our day and the firsts in every area of our lives like money, careers, and the good things we invest our hearts in. If someone examined your calendar over a period of 7 days, what patterns would you see that indicates who you are, what is most important to you, and what you stand for? Are the things that are consuming the majority of your time glorifying to God? Or, is your day designed for self-glorification?

Growing in Christ requires understanding that anything or anyone that moves us in opposition to "the better part" has to decrease. What makes us more in the image of Christ must grow. Some us may simply need to identify a place for prayer. A sacred quiet place for us to spend time with God, engage in conversation with Him, and read our Bible is a great place to start. Some people may need to stop doing life alone and join a group of spiritually like-minded people that enjoy sharing testimonies of God's work in their life. The point is, if your heart desires to grow closer to the Lord, then your actions will reflect change in areas that demonstrate you are more Christ-like and less culture like! Some of us need to ask the Lord to point out people around us that need prayer and to see His Power at work in us! God will always answer and the power of the Holy Spirit is already in you to obey and be part of helping others the way Christ did. 1 John 4:4 says, "You, dear children, are from God and have overcome them, because the one who is in you is greater than the one who is in the world." A walk with Christ reflects experiences that demonstrate He overcomes! Have you seen God do transforming work in your life and the lives of those around you? James 4:3 says, "When you ask, you do not receive, because you ask with wrong motives, that you may spend what you get on your pleasures." God knows what our real motives are when we seek Him and ask for rewards. But if you ask God to perform supernatural work in your life that is not for your own gain or glory, and you believe in your heart this is possible, He will answer!

#3. The Social Area of Our Life:

A race run in grace filled shoes should look like that of a centipede marathon. The definition is "A pacing activity that teaches running at a controlled pace in unity." In some centipede races, the runners are actually connected at the hip or shoulders with rope or tape to maintain an equal pace. The purpose of the centipede strategy is to keep the group together. Groups that run together usually finish together and hold one another accountable. Another benefit is that runners that run together and pace themselves usually have more endurance to run for a longer period of time. Your race as a believer is no different. You need to be surrounded by people that have received the same gift you have and run together towards the same vision for victory in your new shoes. The story of God's grace in your life is designed for a purpose beyond just you, which is to reach others far from Him. If you are living life in isolation, then you are not maximizing the potential and purpose of your testimony. And, according to scripture, sharing our faith is our high calling. Scripture says, "They triumphed over him by the blood of the Lamb and by the word of their testimony; they did not love their lives so much as to shrink from death." It is by demonstration of our faith, the race we run in our grace filled shoes, that we are commanded to be fruitful and multiply. The race is not beneficial if we do not share with others about the gift of his Grace that we have received.

So a person that has received the gift of His Grace and is running in grace filled shoes is telling their story, celebrating their story and others' stories of grace. The social behavior of a grace filled shoes runner manifests in whom gathers (race) together, how frequently we run, and what we do when we run. A person in relationship with Jesus Christ is actively aware of others needs around them and these needs are manifested and lifted up to Christ in their prayer life. A person racing in grace filled shoes to look more like Christ is serving others without being tied to an outcome that is for self-glory or gain. In fact, we grace filled runners are anxious to serve, run alongside with, and celebrate with others. This, like a centipede marathon, is a slow paced evolving change in the way we live our lives. The point is, people running in grace filled shoes begin to change the way they race, where they race to, how they look when they run, who they run with, and become burdened for those that are not in the race at all. When you receive the gift of His Grace and begin a relationship with Christ, change will happen that shows you are running with love, purpose, and passion. For some it may be as simple as having a desire to read your Bible. For others, it may be a desire to mentoring or discipleship, such as joining a men's breakfast or a home group. For some people, it may be asking the person next to you at Walgreens if you can pray for them.

Keri Ann Unsworth

#4. The Financial Area Of Our Life:

Matthew 6:21 "Where your treasure
is, there your heart is also"

Have you ever really given deep thought to the truth in this verse? It is spiritually impossible to say you love Jesus Christ and belong to the Lord, but you are not investing in the things that are important to Christ, according to what is acceptable and pleasing to Him. As a person that went from a nice income to flat broke in a matter of days, I have my own testimony regarding what God has taught me about money. One thing that my mentor has taught me is that I should never teach or share beliefs beyond where I have credibility and experience in life. Well, in the financial area I certainly have gained some credibility.

One major part of the testimony of the transformation we experience when we fully surrender to His Plan above our own is who (Keri's plan) and where (position and paycheck) I was before versus who (Christ surrendered) and where (totally reliant on God for income) I am now.

I had no idea at all how much I had manipulated my financial situation to make me look like God was first in my life. First of all, at work I was very vocal about the Lord and my passion for charitable giving. However, I was quick to spend $800.00 at a time in a matter of minutes at the boutiques on Saturday. Frankly, I had too much money and

I was not a good steward of it regardless of what it seemed. Second, I believed that since I donated so much that it was okay to miss a tithe every now and then. After all, most people that I knew did not even tithe or donate so I was better than them!! Well, folks, that is a cultural lie from the enemy and our finances never shaped up regardless of how much more money I made. We were in the red all the time!! At the time, my husband did not understand tithing so I used his position on money to spend more and give less to the church. Our position on finances was in direct opposition to what God's word says. Scripture in Malachi 3:10 says, "Bring the **whole tithe** into the storehouse, that there may be food in my house. Test me in this," says the Lord Almighty, "and see if I will not throw open the floodgates of heaven and pour out so much blessing that there will not be room enough to store it."

Scripture also says, in Mark 12:41-44:
"Jesus sat down opposite the place where the offerings were put and watched the crowd putting their money into the temple treasury. Many rich people threw in large amounts. But a poor widow came and put in two very small copper coins, worth only a fraction of a penny.

Calling his disciples to him, Jesus said, "I tell you the truth, this poor widow has put more into the treasury than all the others. They all gave out of their wealth; but she, out of her poverty, put in everything—all she had to live on."

In a nutshell, my giving simply reflected that I had a heart for me rather than a heart for God. My spending and my checkbook reflected that I thought first about fashion, others opinions of me, and feeling good than I did about God's plan for our money. Instead of praying for God to open my husband's eyes to tithing and to give him a biblical understanding and desire to tithe, I just used his position to justify my bad behavior. I grew up in a house that tithed and another lie the enemy used to justify my behavior "It didn't work for your parents!".

But when we receive the gift of His Grace, He starts to change the way we finance our shoes to run a grace filled race. Our giving becomes an outpouring of our love for Him and gratitude for His love for us. And I realized that if it were not for the local church, then I may not even have received this gift in my life. There is no better investment to return thankfulness to God than the local church where the gospel is furthered and God's promise is there for all generations to come (Genesis 9:12).

Romans 12:1 *Therefore, I urge you, brothers, in view of God's mercy, to offer your bodies as living sacrifices, holy and pleasing to God—this is your spiritual act of worship.*

Jon and I had nowhere to turn. He did not make enough at this point to cover our mortgage. We tried to handle it on our own for a few months. We just got deeper in debt. I blew through my 401k in complete denial that I would have to seriously change our standard of living. I realized that God could not position Jon to lead our home financially unless I was believing and praying and taking faith prompted action to take this seriously. We enrolled in a financial budget class at church and immediately followed up with monthly counseling sessions. We cut out cable, eating out, and began praying that God would relieve us of a car payment. We surrendered every material thing over to Him and with a pure heart, acknowledged and understood that everything we have is from the Lord. "Thy will be done". In 2 years, still completely reliant on God, Jon got a new position and two raises. We paid off $8,000.00 in debt, and we never question where the Lord is taking us. We have no idea one month to another where my business income will come from or what it will be. But God has provided and met our needs and we never look back on what we used to have or what we used to do. We have never missed a tithe and the crazy thing about that is my income was reduced by more than half! We give more now even beyond our tithe frequently and God always shows up in our lives! Our hearts are positioned for His Plan and not for our gain or for more things. We always have just enough. I believe that God will provide us "the more" once we demonstrate we can surely be trusted with little. I never want to be that lady at the boutique again. And ironically, I find it very difficult now to buy anything! Even when it is something I need, I pray and I sleep on it and get into agreement with my husband first. Luke 16:10 *"Whoever can be trusted with very little can also be trusted with much, and whoever is dishonest with very little will also be dishonest with much.*

Through our journey, we have learned that a pure heart wanting more is so that we can serve others more by giving away what we have. The pursuit of what God has called us to do is first, above what our paycheck or commitments mean to us. We evaluate ourselves prayerfully and make sure that we are always surrendered and reliant on His plan above what we think we need or want. We trust wholly in Ephesians 3:20 and our lives have manifested how faithful God is!

Our financial accounts are reflections of the level of belief we have in His Word. Jon and I look at our bank transactions often and have to cut things out sometimes when it starts to look like we are doing too much of something like iTunes or Apple TV. Because we know that what we spend our time doing and thinking is what we treasure and we want our lives to reflect that our hearts are purposed for Him and our race to further the gospel and reach people far from God is real. One of the reasons I believe there is so much emphasis on money and good stewardship in the Bible is because money and our finances have more power to negatively impact each core area in a significant way. Acts 8:15 shows us "The overcoming Christian life is where the King has dominion", Robert Morris in "Power For Living A Supernatural Life" http://www.faithchannel.com/watch/ondemand/power-for-living-a-supernatural-life – says our hearts are designed to be the dominion for Jesus. If Jesus is enough and you are sold out in pursuit of His calling on your life, then your heart is positioned to release anything that stands in the way of your spiritual growth. The investments we are making show where our hearts are positioned.

The end of this book is just the beginning of your walk!
Put on Your Grace Filled Shoes

I hope that experiencing this written journey has helped you seek the Lord and identify what you can receive from Christ to live God's best for your life. My heart for you is that you immerse your mind, body, and spirit in God's Word and ask Him to show you who you are in Christ. You can never spend too much time reading His Word, on your knees in His Presence asking for His guidance. There are no qualifications needed to get on your knees before Him and read His Word. Any person at any time under any circumstance can go before the Throne of Grace and ask for His Grace, receive it, and begin your walk. Now… go put on your shoes!

Printed in the United States
By Bookmasters